THE CONTEMPORARY CHRISTIAN SONG BOOK

www.brentwoodbenson.com

© MMXI Brentwood-Benson Music Publishing, 2555 Meridian Blvd., Suite 100, Franklin, TN 37067. All Rights Reserved. Unauthorized Duplication Prohibited.

Above All

Words and Music by
PAUL BALOCHE and LENNY LEBLANC

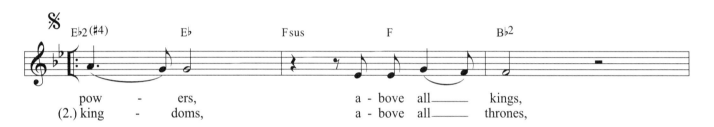

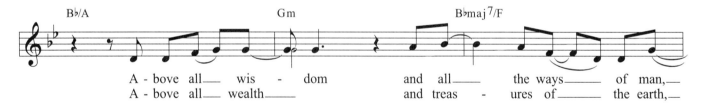
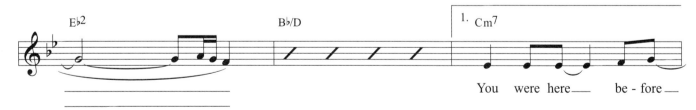

© Copyright 1999 (Arr. © Copyright 2010) Integrity's Hosanna! Music (ASCAP)
(c/o Integrity Media, Inc., 1000 Cody Road, Mobile, AL 36695) / Lensongs Publishing (ASCAP).
All rights reserved. International copyright secured. Used by permission. Reprinted by permission of Hal Leonard Corporation.

Adonai

Words and Music by
DON KOCH, LORRAINE FERRO
and STEPHANIE LEWIS

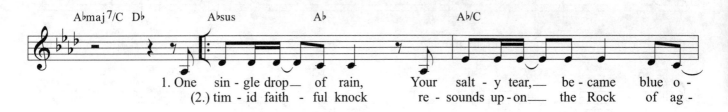

1. One sin-gle drop of rain, Your salt-y tear, be-came blue o-
(2.) tim-id faith-ful knock re-sounds up-on the Rock of ag-

-cean. One ti-ny grain of sand be-
-es. One trem-bling heart and soul be-

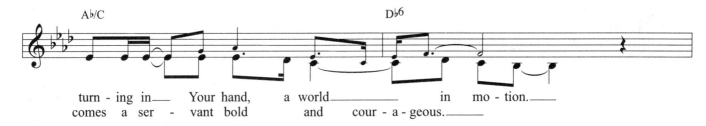

turn-ing in Your hand, a world in mo-tion.
comes a ser-vant bold and cour-a-geous.

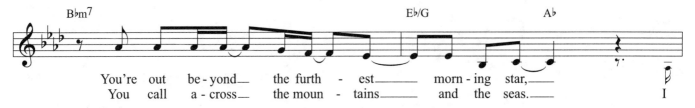

You're out be-yond the furth-est morn-ing star, I
You call a-cross the moun-tains and the seas.

close e-nough to hold me in Your arms. Ad-o-
an-swer from the deep-est part of me.

nai, I lift up my heart, and I cry,

© Copyright 1997 Bridge Building, a division of Brentwood-Benson Music Publishing (BMI) (Licensing through Music Services) /
Birdwing Music (ASCAP) / Sparrow Song (BMI) (Both administered by EMI CMG Publishing) / Dayspring Music, LLC.
All rights reserved. Used by permission.

Adore

Words and Music by
BRENT BOURGEOIS and CHRIS EATON

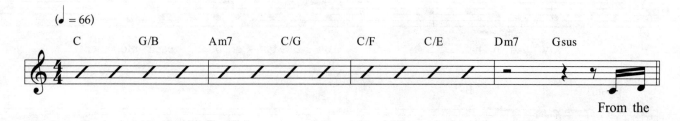

mo - ment You o - pened up my eyes, I've seen the

world in a dif - f'rent light. From the

dawn to the set - ting sun, I am o - ver -

whelmed by all that You have done. A - dore,

a - dore, a - dore, Je - sus, I a - dore You. Ooo

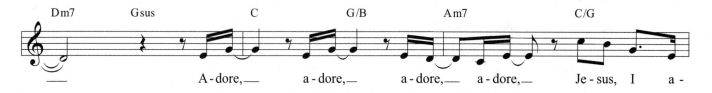
A - dore, a - dore, a - dore, a - dore, Je - sus, I a -

© Copyright 2000 ADC Music (Administered by Wordspring Music, LLC) / Wordspring Music, LLC /
SGO Music Publishing LTD (Administered by Dayspring Music, LLC) / Dayspring Music, LLC.
All rights reserved. Used by permission.

All That I Am

Words and Music by
MARC DODD, MATT FUQUA,
JOSH HAVENS and BRAD WIGG

© Copyright 2005 Smells Like Music / Screaming Mimes Music (ASCAP) (All rights administered by Simpleville Music, Inc.). All rights reserved. Used by permission.

Alive, Forever, Amen

Words and Music by
TRAVIS COTTRELL, DAVID MOFFITT
and SUE C. SMITH

© Copyright 2003 (Arr. © Copyright 2010) New Spring, a division of Brentwood-Benson Music Publishing /
CCTB Music (ASCAP) (Licensing through Music Services) / First Hand Revelation Music (Administered by Integrity's Hosanna! Music) /
Integrity's Hosanna! Music (ASCAP) (c/o Integrity Media, Inc., 1000 Cody Road, Mobile, AL 36695).
All rights reserved. International copyright secured. Used by permission. Reprinted by permission of Hal Leonard Corporation.

All Because of Jesus

Words and Music by
STEVE FEE

Giv - er of ev - 'ry breath— I breathe,— Au - thor of all—

——— e - ter - ni - ty,— Giv - er of ev - 'ry per - fect thing,—

—— to You be the glo - ry. Mak - er of heav -

- en and— of earth,— no one can com - pre - hend— Your worth.—

—— King o - ver all— the u - ni - verse,— to You be the glo -

© Copyright 2007 Worship Together Music / Sixsteps BMI Designee (BMI) / Levi Bear Music (ASCAP) (Administered by EMI CMG Publishing).
All rights reserved. Used by permission.

All My Praise

Words and Music by
AUDREY HATCHER

Audience of One

Words and Music by
MICHAEL WEAVER

© Copyright 2002 Word Music, LLC. All rights reserved. Used by permission.

Beautiful One

Words and Music by
TIM HUGHES

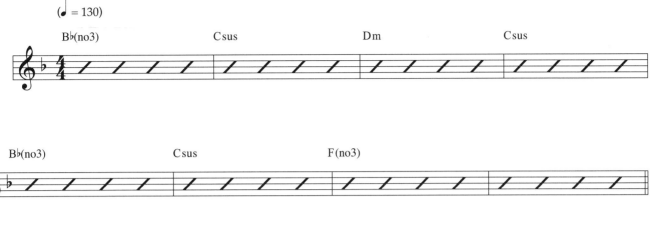

© Copyright 2002 Thankyou Music (PRS) (Administered worldwide by EMI CMG Publishing excluding Europe which is administered by kingswaysongs.com).
All rights reserved. Used by permission.

52

Butterfly Kisses

By His Wounds

Words and Music by
DAVID NASSER
and MAC POWELL

pierced for our trans-gres-sions; He was crushed for our sins. The

pun-ish-ment that brought us peace was up-on Him. And

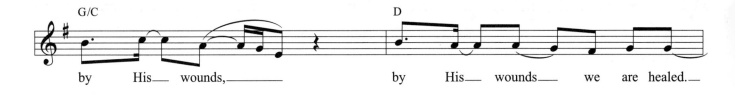
by His wounds, by His wounds we are healed.

He was / We are healed

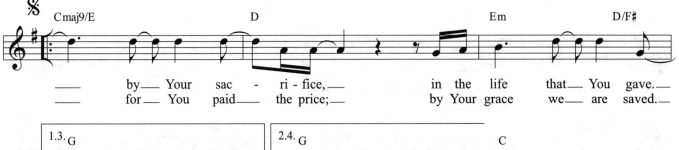
by Your sac-ri-fice, in the life that You gave.
for You paid the price; by Your grace we are saved.

We are healed; We are saved.

© Copyright 2007 Meaux Mercy / Redemptive Art Music (BMI) / Consuming Fire Music (ASCAP) (Administered by EMI CMG Publishing). All rights reserved. Used by permission.

Call on Jesus

Words and Music by
NICOLE C. MULLEN

I'm so ver-y or-di-

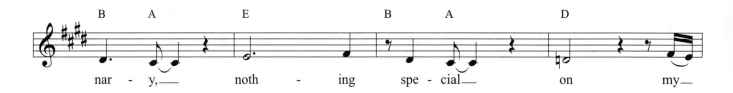

nar-y, noth-ing spe-cial on my

own. Oh, I have nev-er

walked on wa-ter, and I have

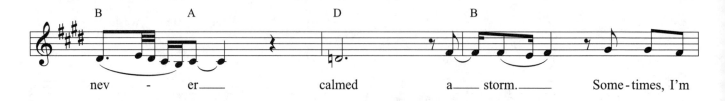

nev-er calmed a storm. Some-times, I'm

© Copyright 2001 Wordspring Music, LLC / Lil Jas Music (SESAC) (Administered by Tunes of R and T Direct c/o Music Services).
All rights reserved. Used by permission.

Cover Me

Words and Music by
BEBO NORMAN

© Copyright 2001 New Spring, a division of Brentwood-Benson Music Publishing / Appstreet Music (ASCAP) (Licensing through Music Services).
All rights reserved. Used by permission.

Cinderella

Words and Music by
STEVEN CURTIS CHAPMAN

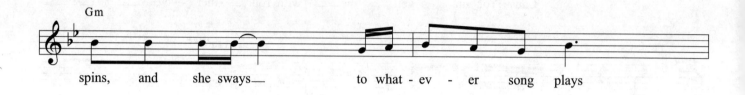

© Copyright 2007 (Arr. © Copyright 2010) Sparrow Song (BMI) (Administered by EMI CMG Publishing) / Primary Wave Brian (Chapman Sp Acct) (BMI).
All rights reserved. Used by permission. Reprinted by permission of Hal Leonard Corporation.

Disappear

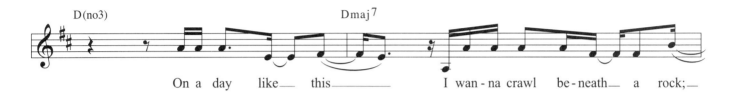
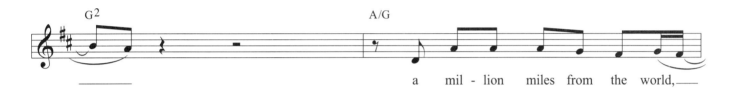
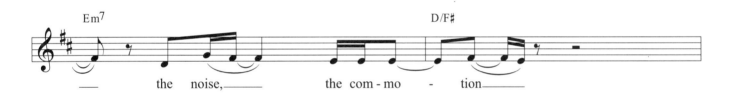

Days of Elijah

Deep Enough to Dream

Words and Music by
CHRIS RICE

La-zy sum-mer af-ter-noon,__ a screened-in porch and noth-in' to do,__ I

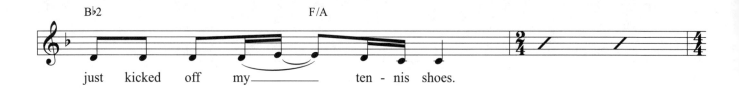

just kicked off my_____ ten-nis shoes.

Slouch-in' in__ a plas-tic chair,__ I'm rak-in' my fin-gers through__ my hair.__ I

close my eyes,__ and I leave 'em there,__ and I yawn__ and sigh__ and slow-

-ly fade a-way.__ Deep e-nough__ to dream__

__ in bril-liant col-ors I__ have nev-er seen. Deep e-nough__ to join__

© Copyright 1997 Clumsy Fly Music (Administered by Word Music, LLC). All rights reserved. Used by permission.

Dive

Words and Music by
STEVEN CURTIS CHAPMAN

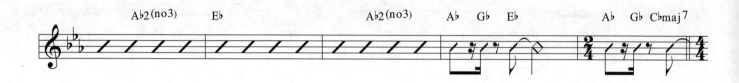

The long a-wait-ed rains— have fall-en hard— up-on— the thirst-y ground;—

—— they've carved their way to where— the wild— and rush-ing riv-er can— be found.—

—— And like the rain,— I have been car-ried here— to where the riv-er flows,—

—— yeah.— My heart is rac-ing, and my

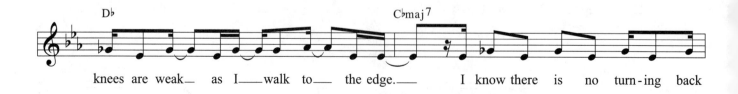

knees are weak— as I— walk to— the edge.— I know there is no turn-ing back

© Copyright 1999 (Arr. © Copyright 2010) Sparrow Song (BMI) (Administered by EMI CMG Publishing) / Primary Wave Brian (Chapman Sp Acct) (BMI).
All rights reserved. Used by permission. Reprinted by permission of Hal Leonard Corporation.

Don't Look at Me

Words and Music by
STACIE ORRICO
and MARK HEIMERMANN

me if you're look-in' for per-fec-tion. Don't look at

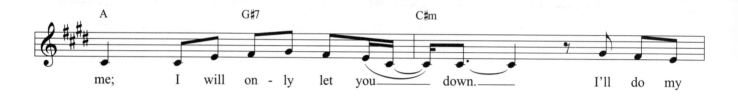

me; I will on-ly let you down. I'll do my

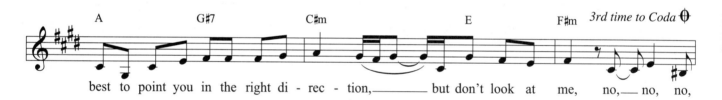

best to point you in the right di-rec-tion, but don't look at me, no, no, no,

don't look at me, look at Him, yeah, yeah. Oh,

1. Some-times I have a fear that you will see a mir-ror
2. It's un-der-stand-a-ble to want a he-ro,

and get the thought that it's the main at-trac-tion.
but peo-ple can't meet all your ex-pec-ta-tions.

© Copyright 2000 Starstruck Music (Administered by EMI CMG Publishing) / Fun Attic Music (ASCAP). All rights reserved. Used by permission.

106

Everything Glorious

East to West

Words and Music by
BERNIE HERMS and MARK HALL

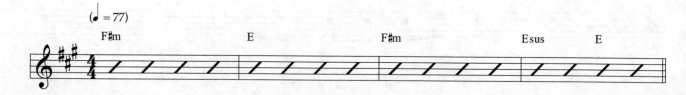
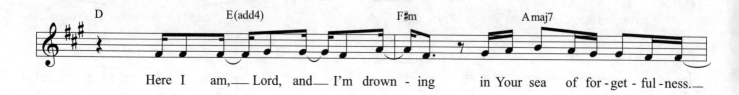

© Copyright 2007 (Arr. © Copyright 2010) Sony/ATV Music Publishing LLC (BMI) / Banahama Tunes (Administered by Word Music, LLC) /
Word Music, LLC / My Refuge Music (BMI) (Administered by EMI CMG Publishing).
Sony/ATV Music Publishing LLC administered by Sony/ATV Music Publishing LLC (8 Music Square West, Nashville, TN 37203).
All rights reserved. Used by permission. Reprinted by permission of Hal Leonard Corporation.

Every Move I Make

Words and Music by
DAVID RUIS

Na, na, na na, na, na, na.

Ev-'ry move I make, I make in You. You make me move, Je-sus.

Ev-'ry breath I take, I breathe in You, oh.

Ev-'ry step I take, I take in You. You are my way, Je-sus.

Ev-'ry breath I take, I breathe in You.

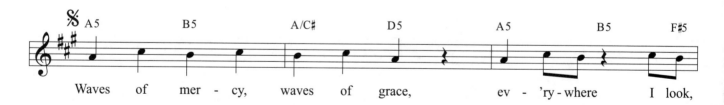
Waves of mer-cy, waves of grace, ev-'ry-where I look,

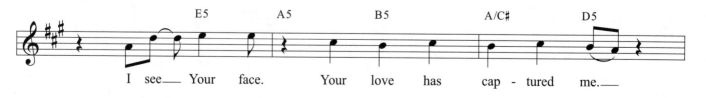
I see Your face. Your love has cap-tured me.

© Copyright 1996 Mercy/Vineyard Publishing (ASCAP) / Vineyard Songs (Canada) (SOCAN) /
ION Publishing (SOCAN) (Administered in North America by Music Services o/b/o Vineyard Music).
All rights reserved. Used by permission.

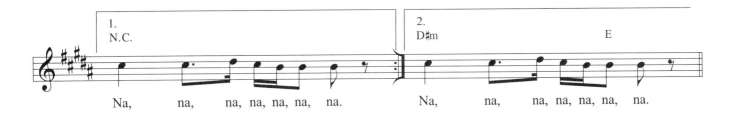

Empty Me

Words and Music by
CHRIS SLIGH, TONY WOOD
and CLINT LAGERBERG

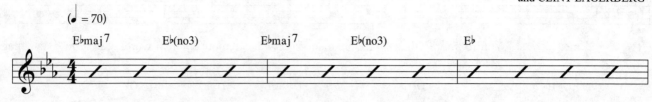

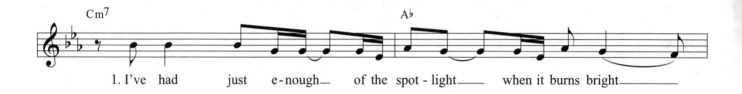

1. I've had just e-nough of the spot-light when it burns bright

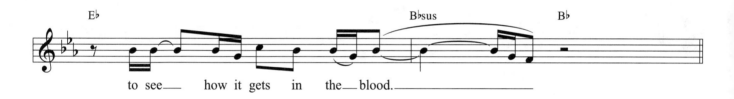

to see how it gets in the blood.

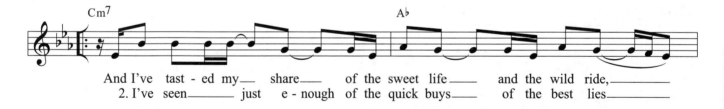

And I've tast-ed my share of the sweet life and the wild ride,
2. I've seen just e-nough of the quick buys of the best lies

and found a lit-tle is not quite e-nough. I
to know how prod-i-gals can be drawn a-way.

know how I can stray and how fast my heart could change.

© Copyright 2008 New Spring, a division of Brentwood-Benson Music Publishing / Row J, Seat 9 Songs (ASCAP) / Brentwood Benson Songs / Kindacrazy Music (BMI) (Licensing through Music Services) / Foolish Tool Music (Administered by Word Music, LLC) / Word Music, LLC.
All rights reserved. Used by permission.

Flood

Words and Music by
DAN HASELTINE, CHARLIE LOWELL,
STEPHEN MASON and MATT ODMARK

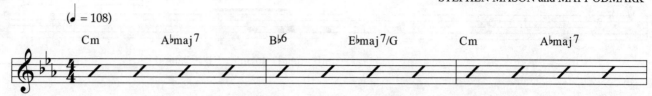

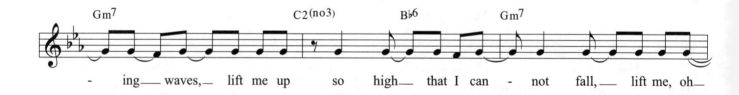

© Copyright 1995 Bridge Building, a division of Brentwood-Benson Music Publishing / Pogostick Music (BMI) (Licensing through Music Services).
All rights reserved. Used by permission.

From the Inside Out

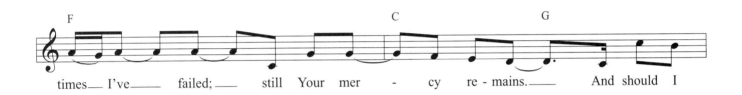

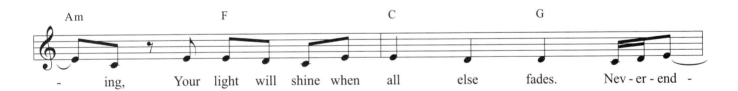
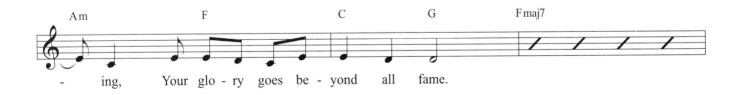

Glory Defined

Words and Music by
JIM COOPER, KENNY LAMB
and JASON ROY

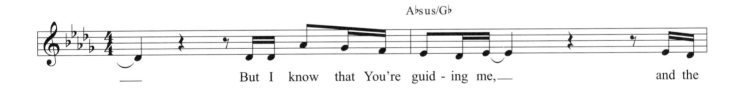

© Copyright 1997 Dayspring Music, LLC / I Give Music (Administered by NEUE WELT MUSIKVERLAG GMBH & CO. KG). All rights reserved. Used by permission.

Give Me Your Eyes

Words and Music by
BRANDON HEATH and JASON INGRAM

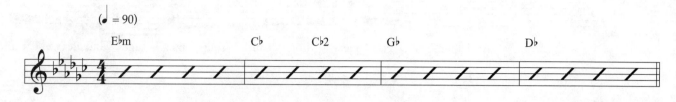

Look down from a bro-ken sky traced out by the cit-y lights,

my world from a mile high, best seat in the house to-night.

Touch down on the cold black-top, hold on for the sud-den stop;

breathe in the fa-mil-iar shock of con-fu-sion and cha-os.

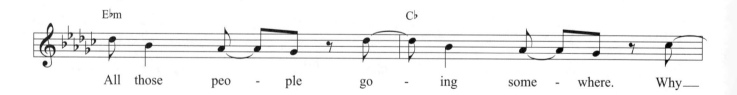
All those peo-ple go-ing some-where. Why

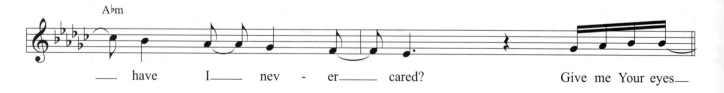
have I nev-er cared? Give me Your eyes

© Copyright 2008 Peertunes, Ltd. / Windsor Way Music / Sony/ATV Music Publishing LLC / Sitka6 Music.
This arrangement © Copyright 2010 Peertunes, Ltd. / Windsor Way Music / Sony/ATV Music Publishing LLC / Sitka6 Music.
All rights for Windsor Way Music administered by Peertunes, Ltd. All rights for Sitka6 Music and
Sony/ATV Music Publishing LLC administered by Sony/ATV Music Publishing LLC (8 Music Square West, Nashville, TN 37203).
International copyright secured. All rights reserved. Reprinted by permission of Hal Leonard Corporation.

God Speaking

Words and Music by
RONNIE FREEMAN

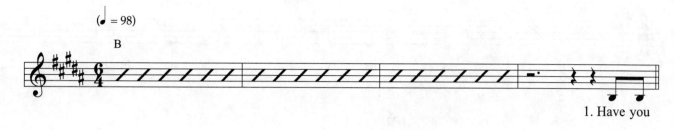

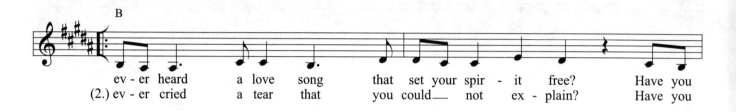

1. Have you ev-er heard a love song that set your spir-it free? Have you
(2.) ev-er cried a tear that you could not ex-plain? Have you

ev-er watched a sun-rise and felt you could-n't breathe? What if it's
ev-er met a strang-er who al-read-y knew your name?

Him? What if it's God speak-ing?

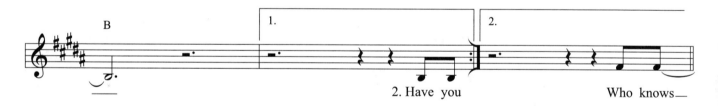

2. Have you Who knows

how He'll get a hold of us, get our at-ten-tion to prove He is e-

nough. He'll do, and He'll use what-

© Copyright 2007 New Spring, a division of Brentwood-Benson Music Publishing / Lehajoes Music (ASCAP) (Licensing through Music Services).
All rights reserved. Used by permission.

Great Light of the World

God with Us

Words and Music by
BART MILLARD, MIKE SCHEUCHZER, JIM BRYSON,
NATHAN COCHRAN, BARRY GRAUL and ROBBY SHAFFER

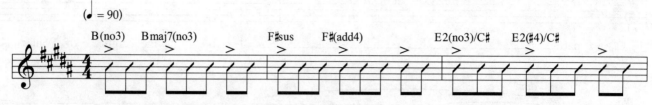

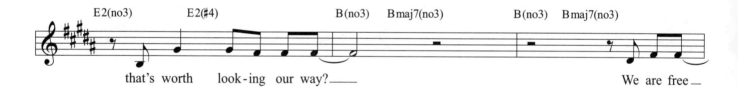
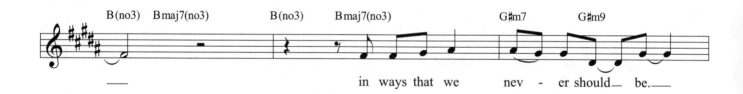

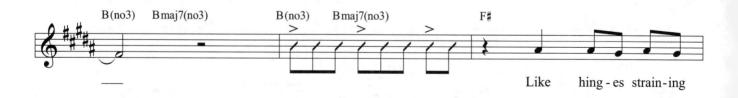

© Copyright 2007 Simpleville Music / Wet As A Fish Music (ASCAP) (All rights administered by Simpleville Music, Inc.). All rights reserved. Used by permission.

He Reigns

Words and Music by
PETER FURLER and STEVE TAYLOR

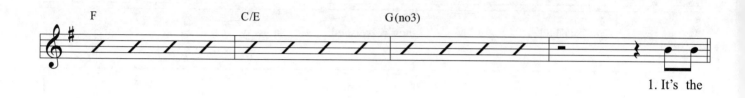

1. It's the song of the redeemed rising from the African plain.
(2.) rise above the four winds, caught up in the heavenly sound.

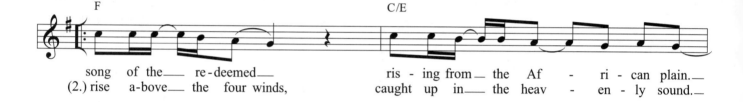

It's the song of the forgiven
Let praises echo from the towers of cathedrals to the

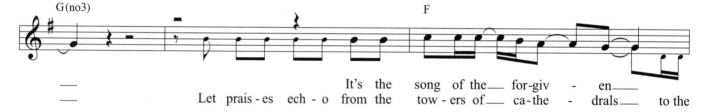

drowning out the Amazon rain, the song of
faithful gathered underground. Of all the songs sung from the

Asian believers filled with God's holy fire.
dawn of creation, some were meant to persist.

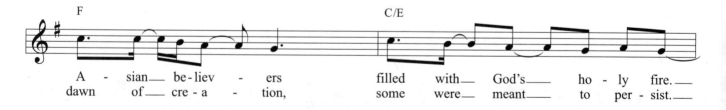

It's ev'ry tribe, ev'ry tongue, ev'ry nation, a
Of all the bells rung from a thousand steeples,

© Copyright 2003 Ariose Music (ASCAP) (Administered by EMI CMG Publishing) / Soylent Tunes (SESAC) (Administered by EverGreen Copyrights).
All rights reserved. Used by permission.

Here I Am to Worship

189

Words and Music by
TIM HUGHES

(♩ = 76)

Light of the world, You stepped down in-to dark-ness,

Track begins with 2 bars percussion

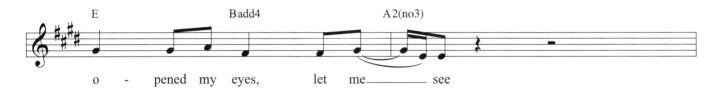

o - pened my eyes, let me see

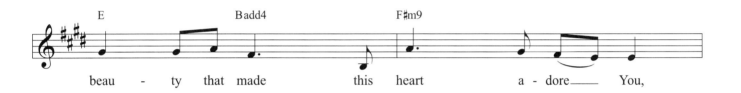

beau - ty that made this heart a - dore You,

hope of a life spent with You. So, here I am to

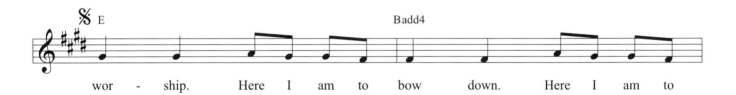

wor - ship. Here I am to bow down. Here I am to

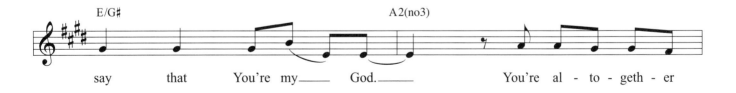

say that You're my God. You're al - to - geth - er

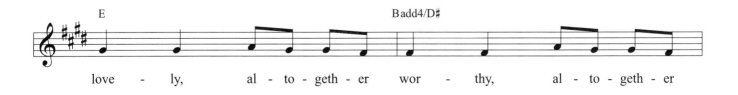

love - ly, al - to - geth - er wor - thy, al - to - geth - er

© Copyright 2001 Thankyou Music (PRS) (Administered worldwide by EMI CMG Publishing excluding Europe which is administered by kingswaysongs.com).
All rights reserved. Used by permission.

Here Is Our King

Here with Me

205

Words and Music by
DAN MUCKALA, BRAD RUSSELL, PETE KIPLEY,
BART MILLARD, JIM BRYSON, NATHAN COCHRAN,
BARRY GRAUL, MIKE SCHEUCHZER and ROBBY SHAFFER

I long for Your embrace

ev-'ry sin-gle day, to meet You in this place

and see You face to face. Will You show

me, reveal Yourself to me?

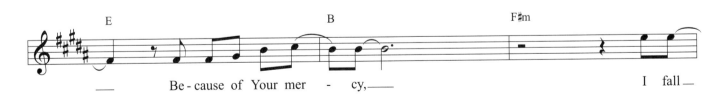

Because of Your mer-cy, I fall

down on my knees. And I can feel Your

© Copyright 2004 Zooki Tunes / Songs From the Indigo Room (Both administered by Wordspring Music, LLC) / Wordspring Music, LLC /
Simpleville Music / Wet As a Fish Music (ASCAP) (Administered by Simpleville Music, Inc.) / Russell Made Music (Administered by Fun Attic).
All rights reserved. Used by permission.

Holy Is Your Name

Words and Music by
STEVE HINDALONG and MARC BYRD

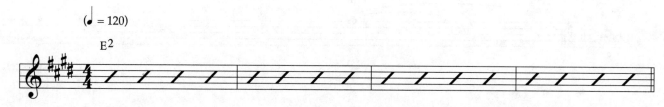

Now I praise You, Lord of all cre-a-tion;

You or-dain the sun to rise and fall.

You scat-ter the stars a-cross the heav-

-ens; and You come close e-nough

to hear me call. Now I want to

say ho-ly is Your name.

© Copyright 2001 New Spring, a division of Brentwood-Benson Music Publishing / Never Say Never Songs (ASCAP)
(Licensing through Music Services) / Storm Boy Music / Meaux Mercy (BMI) (Administered by EMI CMG Publishing).
All rights reserved. Used by permission.

Holy

Words and Music by
NICHOLE NORDEMAN and MARK HAMMOND

© Copyright 2002 Ariose Music (ASCAP) (Administered by EMI CMG Publishing) / Mark Hammond Music (ASCAP) (Administered by EverGreen Copyrights).
All rights reserved. Used by permission.

Holy Is the Lord

Words and Music by
CHRIS TOMLIN and LOUIE GIGLIO

We stand and lift up our hands, for the joy

of the Lord is our strength.

We bow down and wor-ship Him now. How great,

how awe-some is He. And to-geth-er we sing;

ev-'ry-one sing.

Ho-ly is the Lord God Al-might-

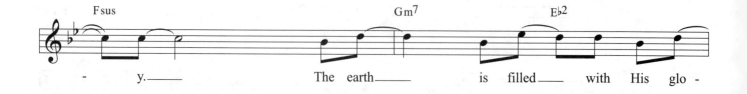
-y. The earth is filled with His glo-

© Copyright 2003 worshiptogether.com Songs / sixsteps Music (ASCAP) (Administered by EMI CMG Publishing). All rights reserved. Used by permission.

Homesick

Words and Music by
BART MILLARD

You're in a better place, I've heard a thou-

-sand times; and at least a thousand times I've rejoiced

for you. But the reason why I'm broken, the

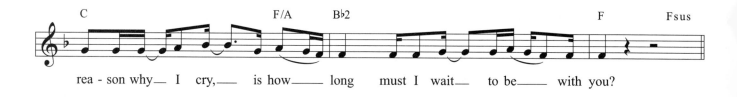

reason why I cry, is how long must I wait to be with you?

I close my eyes, and I see your face. If home's where my heart is, then I'm

out of place. Lord, won't You give me strength to make it through somehow?

© Copyright 2004 Simpleville Music (ASCAP) (All rights administered by Simpleville Music, Inc.). All rights reserved. Used by permission.

How Great Is Our God

Words and Music by
CHRIS TOMLIN, JESSE REEVES
and ED CASH

© Copyright 2004 worshiptogether.com Songs / sixsteps Music (ASCAP)
(Administered by EMI CMG Publishing) / Alletrop Music (BMI) (Administered by Music Services).
All rights reserved. Used by permission.

I Am

Words and Music by
MARK SCHULTZ

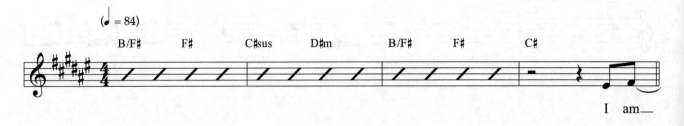

© Copyright 2005 Crazy Romaine Music (ASCAP) (Administered by The Loving Company). All rights reserved. Used by permission.

I Am Free

Words and Music by
JON EGAN

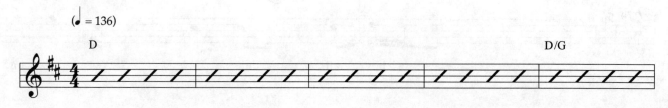

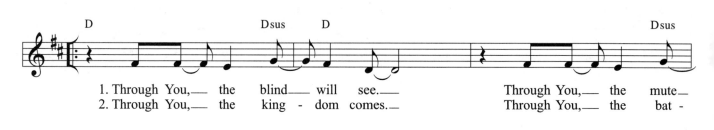

1. Through You, the blind will see. Through You, the mute will sing.
2. Through You, the king-dom comes. Through You, the bat-tle's won.

Through You, the dead will rise.
Through You, I'm not a-fraid.

Through You, all hearts will praise.
Through You, the price is paid.

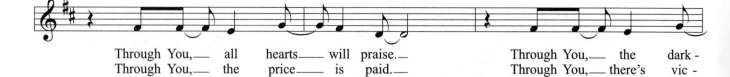

Through You, the dark-ness flees.
Through You, there's vic-to-ry.

Through You, my heart screams, "I am free!"
Be-cause of You, my heart screams, "I am free!"

© Copyright 2004 Vertical Worship Songs (ASCAP) (Administered by Integrity's Hosanna! Music). This arrangement © Copyright 2010
Vertical Worship Songs (ASCAP) (Administered by Integrity's Hosanna! Music) (c/o Integrity Media, Inc., 1000 Cody Road, Mobile, AL 36695).
All rights reserved. International copyright secured. Used by permission. Reprinted by permission of Hal Leonard Corporation.

I Believe

Words and Music by
MAC POWELL, TAI ANDERSON, BRAD AVERY,
DAVID CARR and MARK LEE

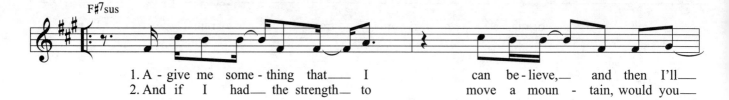

1. A - give me some-thing that I can be-lieve, and then I'll
2. And if I had the strength to move a moun-tain, would you

— share it with the world for ev-'ry-one to see.
— be a - mazed by all of my a - bil - i - ties?

A - take a - way the dark - ness, all the pain and sad - ness;
I guess it would not mean much if I did - n't have love,

— I know it's You that put this light in - side of me.
— and this is what I real - ly want you all to see.

I be - lieve in a faith that's strong. And

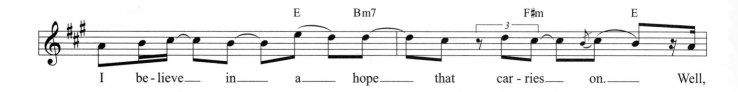

I be - lieve in a hope that car - ries on. Well,

© Copyright 2004 Consuming Fire (Administered by EMI CMG Publishing). All rights reserved. Used by permission.

I Can Only Imagine

Words and Music by
BART MILLARD

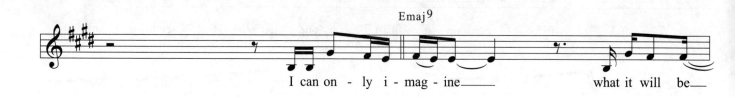

I can on-ly i-mag-ine_____ what it will be_____

_____ like_____ when I walk_____ by Your side._____

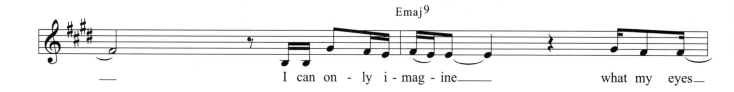

_____ I can on-ly i-mag-ine_____ what my eyes_____

_____ will see_____ when Your face_____ is be-fore_____

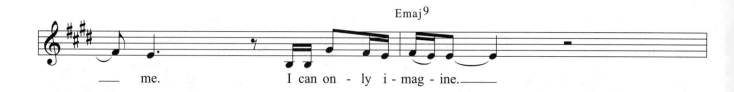

_____ me. I can on-ly i-mag-ine._____

Sur-

© Copyright 2001 Simpleville Music (ASCAP) (All rights administered by Simpleville Music, Inc.). All rights reserved. Used by permission.

If We Are the Body

Indescribable

Words and Music by
JESSE REEVES and LAURA STORY

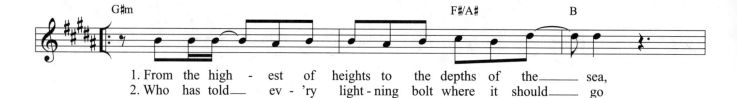

1. From the high-est of heights to the depths of the sea,
2. Who has told ev-'ry light-ning bolt where it should go

cre-a-tion's re-veal-ing Your maj-es-
or seen heav-en-ly store-hous-es lad-en with

ty. From the col-ors of
snow? Who im-ag-ined the

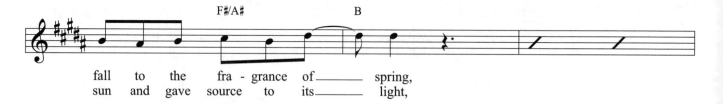

fall to the fra-grance of spring,
sun and gave source to its light,

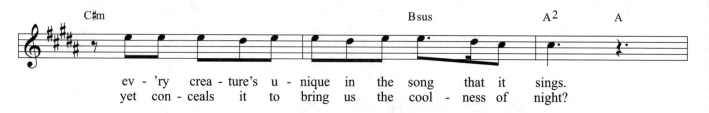

ev-'ry crea-ture's u-nique in the song that it sings.
yet con-ceals it to bring us the cool-ness of night?

© Copyright 2004 worshiptogether.com Songs / sixsteps Music / Gleaning Publishing (ASCAP) (Administered by EMI CMG Publishing).
All rights reserved. Used by permission.

In Christ Alone

279

Words and Music by
DON KOCH and SHAWN CRAIG

In Christ a-lone___ will I glo-ry, though I could pride___ my-self___ in bat-tles won.___ For I've been blessed be-yond meas-ure, and by His strength___ a-lone___ I o-ver-come. Oh, I could stop and count___ suc-cess-es like dia-monds in___ my hands,___ but those tro-phies___ could not e-qual to the grace by which___ I___

© Copyright 1990 New Spring, a division of Brentwood-Benson Music Publishing (ASCAP) (Licensing through Music Services). All rights reserved. Used by permission.

Joy

King of Glory

Words and Music by
MAC POWELL, TAI ANDERSON, BRAD AVERY,
DAVID CARR and MARK LEE

© Copyright 2000 New Spring, a division of Brentwood-Benson Music Publishing (ASCAP)
(Licensing through Music Services) / Vandura 2500 Songs (ASCAP) (Administered by EMI CMG Publishing).
All rights reserved. Used by permission.

Let Us Pray

Words and Music by
STEVEN CURTIS CHAPMAN

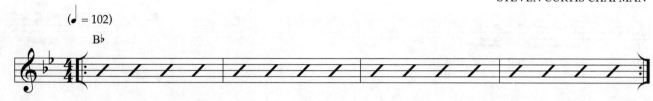

1. I hear you say your heart is ach-ing; you've got trou-ble in the mak-
2. So when we feel the Spir-it mov-ing, prompt-ing, prod-ding and be-hoov-

- ing, and you ask if I'll be pray-ing for you, please.
- ing, there is no time to be los-ing; let us pray.

And in keep-ing with con-ven-tion, I'll say yes, with good in-ten-
Let the Fa-ther hear us say-ing what we need to be con-vey-

- tions to pray lat-er, mak-ing men-tion of your needs.
- ing. E-ven while this song is play-ing, let us pray.

But since we have this mo-ment here at heav-en's door,
And just be-cause we say the word, "A-men,"

we should start knock-ing now. What are we wait-ing for? Let us pray,
it does-n't mean this con-ver-sa-tion needs to end.

© Copyright 1996 (Arr. © Copyright 2010) Sparrow Song (BMI) (Administered by EMI CMG Publishing) / Primary Wave Brian (Chapman Sp Acct) (BMI).
All rights reserved. Used by permission. Reprinted by permission of Hal Leonard Corporation.

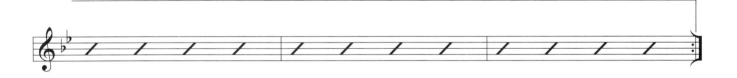

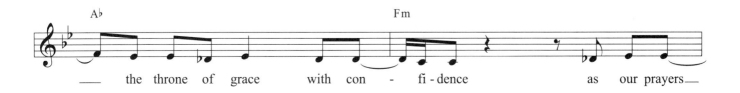

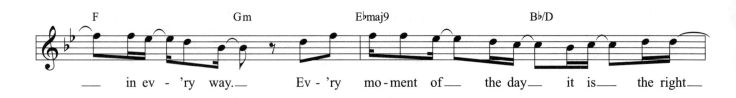
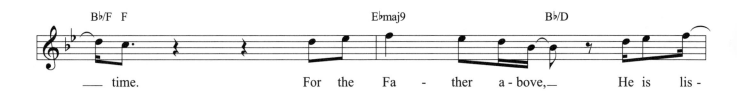
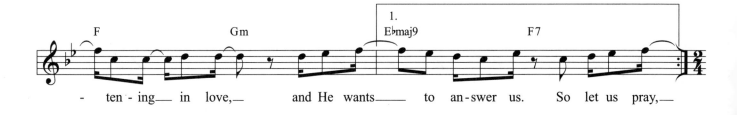
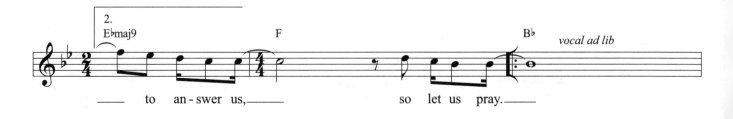

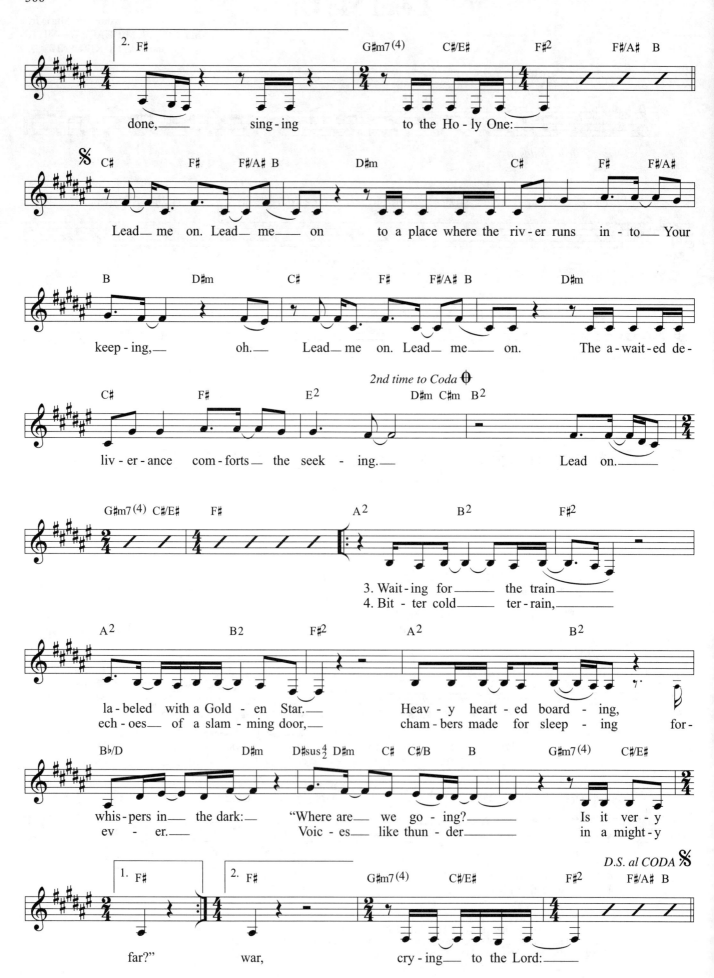

Leaving 99

Words and Music by BEN CISSELL, BOB HERDMAN, MARK STUART, TYLER BURKUM and WILL MCGINNISS

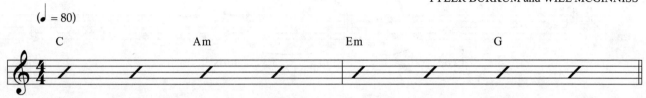

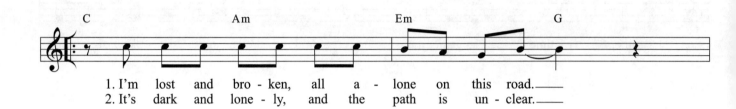

1. I'm lost and bro-ken, all a-lone on this road.
2. It's dark and lone-ly, and the path is un-clear.

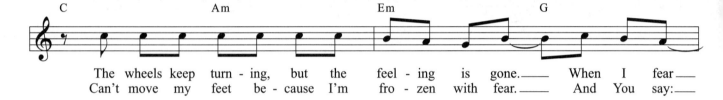

The wheels keep turn-ing, but the feel-ing is gone. When I fear
Can't move my feet be-cause I'm fro-zen with fear. And You say:

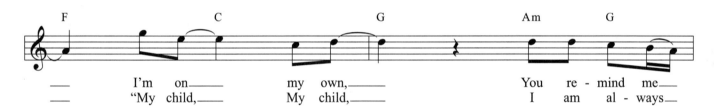

— I'm on my own, You re-mind me
— "My child, My child, I am al-ways

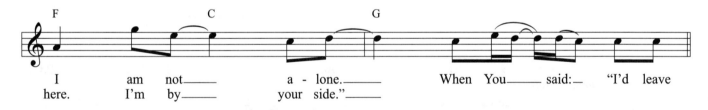

I am not a-lone. When You said: "I'd leave
here. I'm by your side."

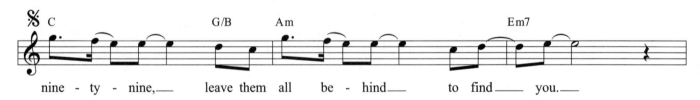

nine-ty nine, leave them all be-hind to find you.

For you a-lone, I'd leave nine-ty nine, leave them all be-hind to find

© Copyright 2003 Flicker USA Publishing / Up in the Mix Music (BMI) / Allen Vaughn and Ray Publishing (ASCAP) (Administered by EMI CMG Publishing).
All rights reserved. Used by permission.

Legacy

Words and Music by
NICHOLE NORDEMAN

© Copyright 2002 Ariose Music (ASCAP) (Administered by EMI CMG Publishing). All rights reserved. Used by permission.

Let My Words Be Few

Words and Music by
MATT REDMAN and BETH REDMAN

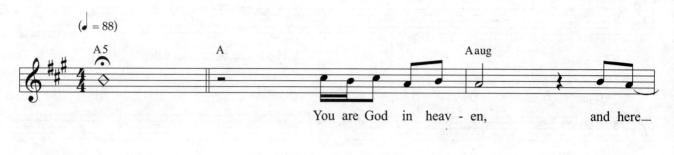
You are God in heav-en, and here

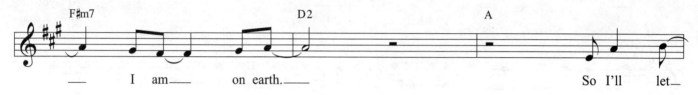
I am on earth. So I'll let

my words be few: Je-

-sus, I am so in love with You.

And I'll stand in awe of You,

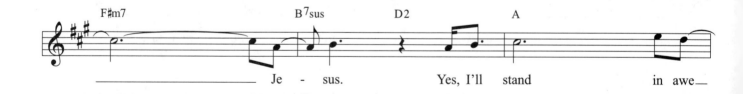
Je-sus. Yes, I'll stand in awe

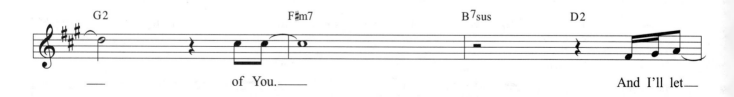
of You. And I'll let

© Copyright 2000 Thankyou Music (PRS) (Administered worldwide by EMI CMG Publishing excluding Europe which is administered by kingswaysongs.com).
All rights reserved. Used by permission.

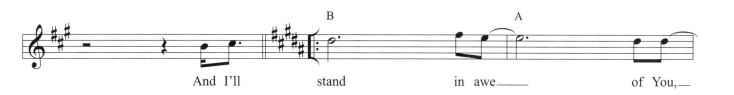
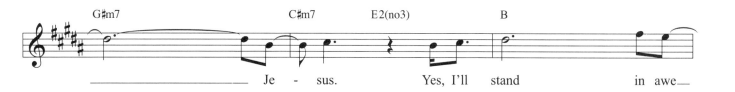

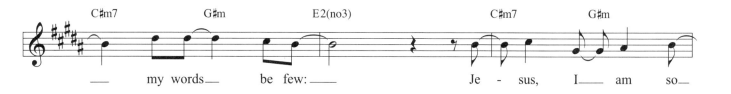
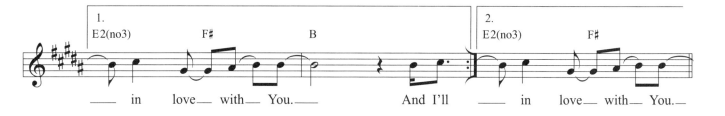

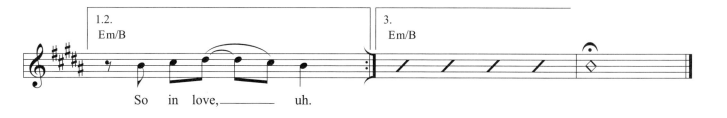

Love Is Here

331

Words and Music by
JASON INGRAM, PHILLIP LARUE, MIKE DONEHEY,
JASON JAMISON and DREW MIDDLETON

Come to the Wa - ter, you who thirst, and you'll thirst

no more. Come to the Fa - ther, you

who work, and you'll work no more.

And all you who la - bor in vain, and to the bro - ken and shamed,

Love is here, Love is now. Love is

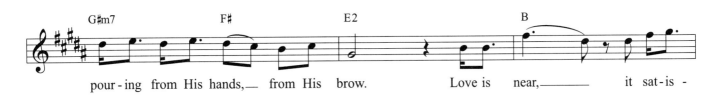

pour - ing from His hands, from His brow. Love is near, it sat - is -

© Copyright 2008, 2009 (Arr. © Copyright 2010) Songs of Razor and Tie / My Maxx Songs / Deeper Still Music Publishing (ASCAP)
(Administered by Songs of Razor and Tie c/o Music Services) / Peertunes, Ltd / Windsor Way Music / Sony/ATV Music Publishing LLC /
Formerly Music / DMiddleton Publishing. All rights for Windsor Way Music administered by Peertunes, Ltd. All rights on behalf of
Sony/ATV Music Publishing LLC and Formerly Music administered by Sony/ATV Music Publishing LLC (8 Music Square West, Nashville, TN 37203).
All rights reserved. International copyright secured. Used by permission.

Made to Worship

Words and Music by
CHRIS TOMLIN, ED CASH
and STEPHAN SHARP

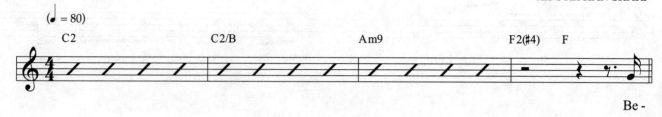

Be- fore the day,___ be- fore the light,___ be-

fore the world___ re- volved___ a- round___ the sun,___

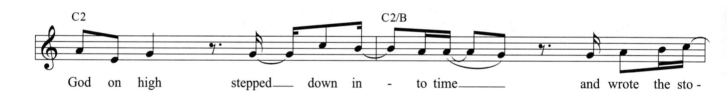
God on high stepped___ down in- to time___ and wrote the sto-

-ry of___ His love___ for ev- 'ry one.___

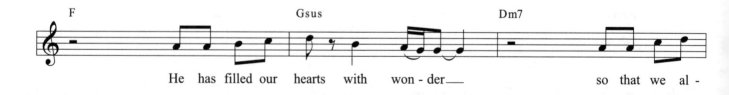
He has filled our hearts with won- der___ so that we al-

-ways re- mem- ber: You and I___ were made___ to wor- ship.

© Copyright 2006 New Spring, a division of Brentwood-Benson Music Publishing / Stenpan Music (ASCAP) (Licensing through Music Services) / worshiptogether.com Songs / sixsteps Music / Vamos Publishing (ASCAP) (Administered by EMI CMG Publishing) / Alletrop Music (BMI) (Administered by Music Services). All rights reserved. Used by permission.

Me and Jesus

Words and Music by
IAN ESKELIN and ADAM AGEE

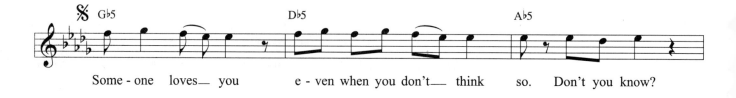

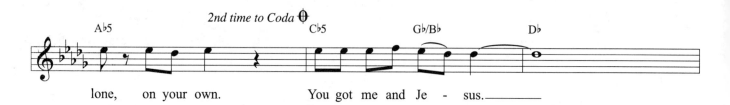

© Copyright 2006 Bridge Building, a division of Brentwood-Benson Music Publishing /
Starshaped Music (BMI) (Licensing through Music Services) / Wordspring Music, LLC.
All rights reserved. Used by permission.

Magnificent Obsession

341

Words and Music by
STEVEN CURTIS CHAPMAN

Lord, You know how much I want to know so much

in the way of an-swers and ex-pla-na-tions.

I have cried and prayed, and still I seem to stay

in the mid-dle of life's com-pli-ca-tions.

All this pur-su-ing leaves me feel-ing like I'm chas-ing down the wind,

© Copyright 2001 (Arr. © Copyright 2010) Sparrow Song (BMI) (Administered by EMI CMG Publishing) / Primary Wave Brian (Chapman Sp Acct) (BMI).
All rights reserved. Used by permission. Reprinted by permission of Hal Leonard Corporation.

Never Alone

Words and Music by
BARLOWGIRL

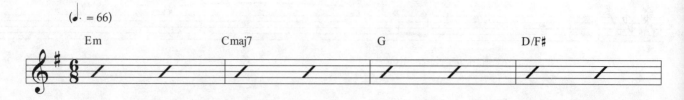

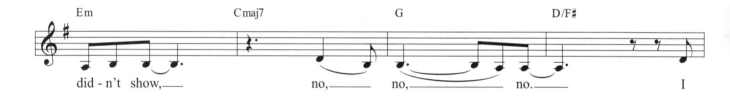

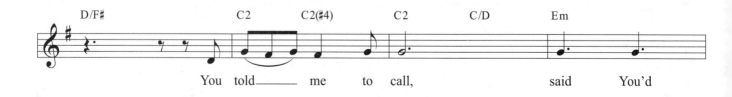

© Copyright 2004 Word Music, LLC. All rights reserved. Used by permission.

Spoken: *And those words that were spoken and written by the apostle Paul, apply just as much to our lives today as they did two thousand years ago when he wrote them. That in our lives, no matter where we could go, or who we could meet, or what we could see, or what we could earn or be given to us, or accomplished, there is nothing in our lives that will ever even come close to the greatness of knowing Jesus Christ, our Lord.*

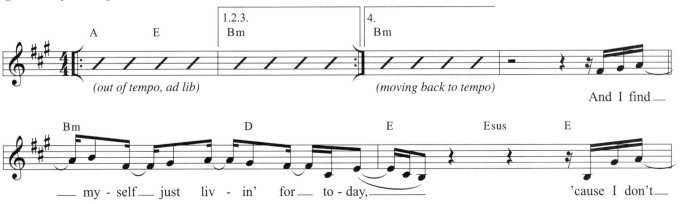

Ocean Floor

Words and Music by
BEN CISSELL, BOB HERDMAN, MARK STUART,
TYLER BURKUM and WILL MCGINNISS

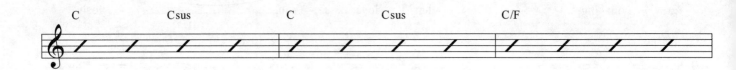

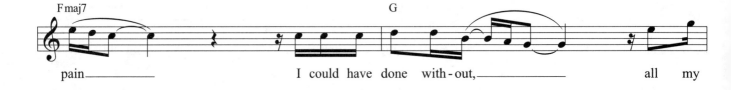

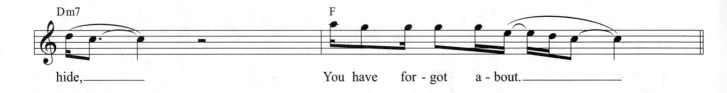

© Copyright 2001 Flicker USA Publishing / Up in the Mix (BMI) / Allen Vaughn and Ray Publishing (ASCAP) (Administered by EMI CMG Publishing).
All rights reserved. Used by permission.

Once Again

381

Words and Music by
MATT REDMAN

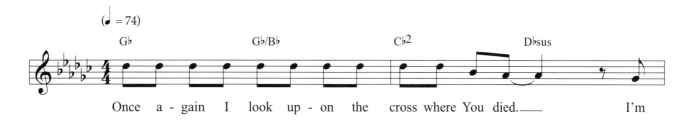

© Copyright 1996 Thankyou Music (PRS) (Administered worldwide by EMI CMG Publishing excluding Europe which is administered by kingswaysongs.com).
All rights reserved. Used by permission.

Open the Eyes of My Heart

393

Words and Music by
PAUL BALOCHE

O-pen the eyes of my heart, Lord. O-pen the eyes of my heart.

I want to see You. I want to

see You. O-pen the eyes of my heart,

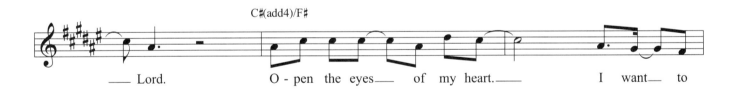
Lord. O-pen the eyes of my heart. I want to

see You. I want to see You,

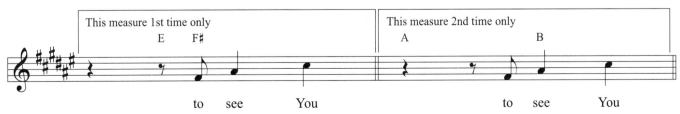
to see You / to see You

© Copyright 1997 Integrity's Hosanna! Music (ASCAP).
This arrangement © Copyright 2010 Integrity's Hosanna! Music (ASCAP) (c/o Integrity Media, Inc., 1000 Cody Road, Mobile, AL 36695).
All rights reserved. International copyright secured. Used by permission. Reprinted by permission of Hal Leonard Corporation.

Praise You in This Storm

405

Words and Music by
MARK HALL and BERNIE HERMS

© Copyright 2005 (Arr. © Copyright 2010) Sony/ATV Music Publishing LLC (BMI) / Banahama Tunes
(Administered by Word Music, LLC) / Word Music, LLC / My Refuge Music (BMI) (Administered by EMI CMG Publishing).
Sony/ATV Music Publishing LLC administered by Sony/ATV Music Publishing LLC (8 Music Square West, Nashville, TN 37203).
All rights reserved. Used by permission. Reprinted by permission of Hal Leonard Corporation.

Psalm 112

Words and Music by
MARK HARRIS and TONY WOOD

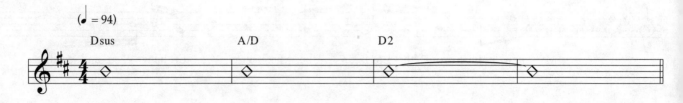
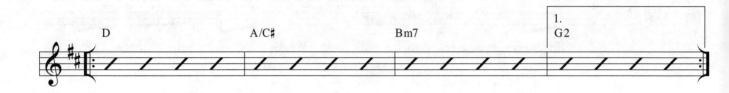

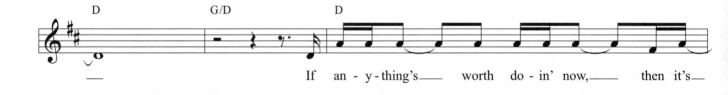
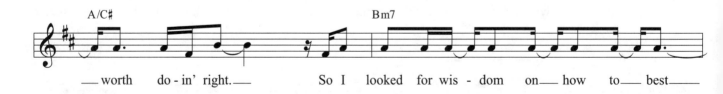

© Copyright 2001 New Spring, a division of Brentwood-Benson Music Publishing (ASCAP) (Licensing through Music Services). All rights reserved. Used by permission.

Revelation Song

Words and Music by JENNIE LEE RIDDLE

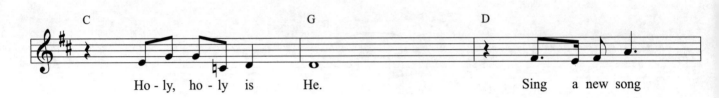
Ho-ly, ho-ly is He. Sing a new song

to Him who sits on heav-en's mer - cy seat.

Ho-ly, ho-ly, ho-ly is the Lord, God Al-might - y,

who was and is and is to come.

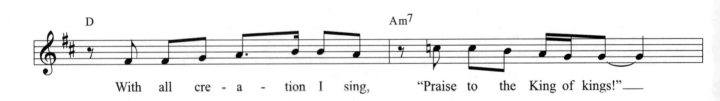
With all cre-a-tion I sing, "Praise to the King of kings!"

You are my ev-'ry-thing, and I will a-dore You.

© Copyright 2004 Gateway Create Publishing (BMI) (Administered by Integrity's Praise! Music). This arrangement © Copyright 2010 Gateway Create Publishing (BMI) (Administered by Integrity's Praise! Music) (c/o Integrity Media, Inc., 1000 Cody Road, Mobile, AL 36695). All rights reserved. International copyright secured. Used by permission. Reprinted by permission of Hal Leonard Corporation.

Show Me Your Glory

Words and Music by
MAC POWELL, TAI ANDERSON, BRAD AVERY,
DAVID CARR, MARK LEE and MARC BYRD

1. I caught a glimpse of Your splen-dor in the cor-ner of my eye;
2. When I climb down the moun-tain and get back to my life,

the most beau-ti-ful thing I've ev-er seen.
I won't set-tle for or-di-nar-y things.

And it was like a flash of light-ning re-flect-ed off the sky,
I'm gon-na fol-low You for-ev-er, for all of my days.

and I know I'll nev-er be the same.
I won't rest till I see You a-gain.

Show me Your glo-ry.

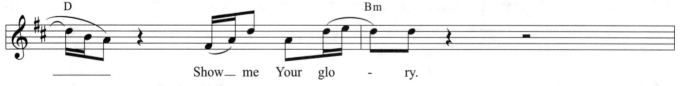

Send down Your pres-ence; I wan-na see Your face.

© Copyright 2001 New Spring, a division of Brentwood-Benson Music Publishing (ASCAP) (Licensing through Music Services) /
Meaux Mercy (BMI) / Vandura 2500 Songs (ASCAP) (Administered by EMI CMG Publishing).
All rights reserved. Used by permission.

So Long, Self

Words and Music by
BART MILLARD, JIM BRYSON, NATHAN COCHRAN,
BARRY GRAUL, MIKE SCHEUCHZER and ROBBY SHAFFER

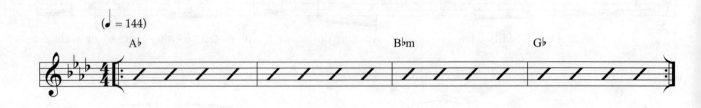

1. Well, if I come across a little bit distant, it's
2. Stop right there, because I know what you're thinking. But

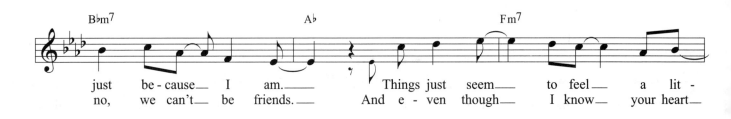

just because I am. Things just seem to feel a lit-
no, we can't be friends. And even though I know your heart

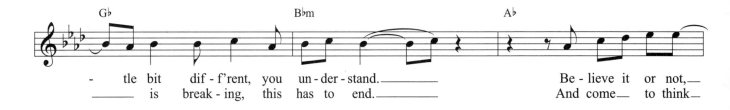

-tle bit diff'rent, you understand. Believe it or not,
is breaking, this has to end. And come to think

but life is not apparently about me anyways.
of it, the blame for all of this simply falls on me

But I have met the One who really is worthy, so let me say:
for wanting something more in life than all of this. Oh, can't you see?

© Copyright 2006 Simpleville Music / Wet As A Fish Music (ASCAP) (All rights administered by Simpleville Music, Inc.). All rights reserved. Used by permission.

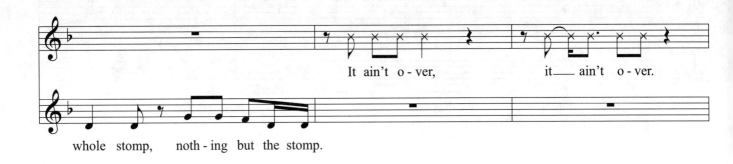
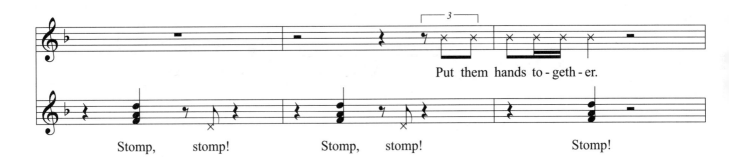

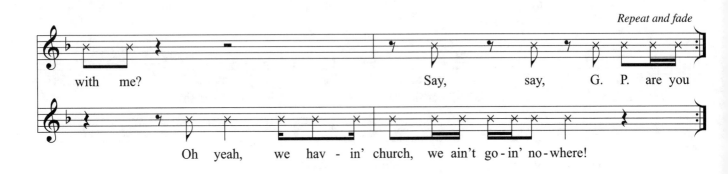

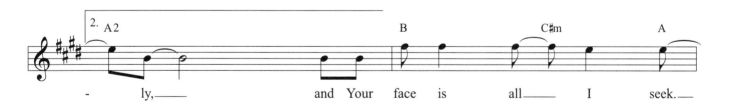
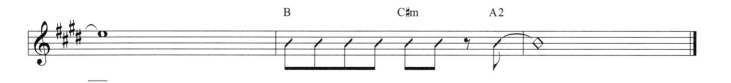

Take You Back

Words and Music by
JEREMY CAMP

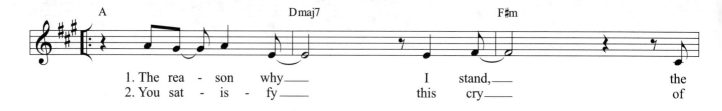

1. The rea-son why_____ I stand,_____ the an-swer lies_____ in You._____ You hung_____ to make_____ me strong, though my praise_____ was few._____
2. You sat-is-fy_____ this cry_____ of what I'm look-ing for,_____ and I'll take_____ all_____ I can_____ and lay it down_____ be-fore_____

When I fall_____ the throne_____

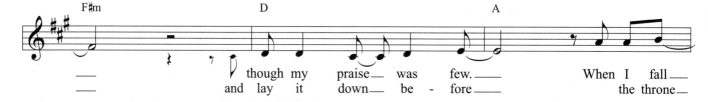

I bring_____ Your name_____ down,_____ but I have found_____ in You_____
of end-less grace_____ now_____ that ra-di-ates_____ what's true._____

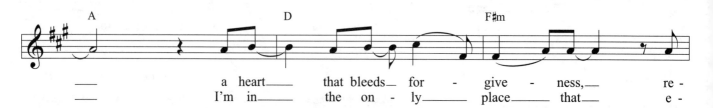

a heart_____ that bleeds_____ for-give-ness,_____ re-
I'm in_____ the on-ly place_____ that_____ e-

© Copyright 2004 Stolen Pride Music / Thirsty Moon River Publishing, Inc. (ASCAP) (Administered by EMI CMG Publishing). All rights reserved. Used by permission.

The Valley Song (Sing of Your Mercy)

483

Words and Music by
DAN HASELTINE, CHARLIE LOWELL, STEPHEN MASON,
MATT ODMARK and AARON SANDS

You have led me to the sad - ness; I have car - ried this pain. On a back bruised, near-ly bro - ken, I'm cry-ing out to You. I will sing of Your mer-cy that leads me through val-leys of sor - row to riv-ers of joy. When death, like a gyp-sy comes to steal what I love, I will still look to the heav - ens. I will still seek Your face. But I fear You aren't lis-ten-ing, be-cause there are no words, just the still - ness and the hun - ger for a faith that as - sures. I will sing of Your mer-cy that leads me through val-leys of

© Copyright 2002 Bridge Building, a division of Brentwood-Benson Music Publishing / Pogostick Music (BMI)
(Licensing through Music Services) / Innocent Smith (ASCAP) (Administered by The Loving Company).
All rights reserved. Used by permission.

There You Go

Words and Music by
AARON TATE

There Will Be a Day

489

Words and Music by
JEREMY CAMP

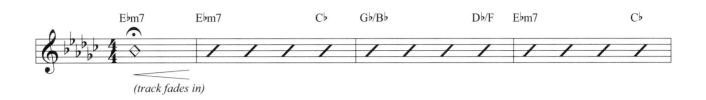
(track fades in)

I try to hold on to this world

with ev-'ry-thing I have, but I feel the weight of what

it brings and the hurt that tries to grab, the man-y trials that seem to nev-

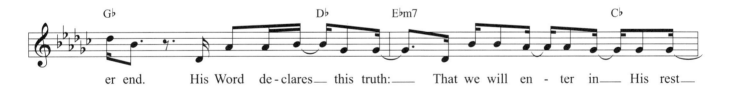
er end. His Word de-clares this truth: That we will en-ter in His rest

with won-ders a-new. But I hold on to this hope

and the prom-ise that He brings, that there will be a place with no

© Copyright 2008 Stolen Pride Music / Thirsty Moon River Publishing, Inc. (ASCAP) (Administered by EMI CMG Publishing). All rights reserved. Used by permission.

This Day

Words and Music by
STEVEN CURTIS CHAPMAN

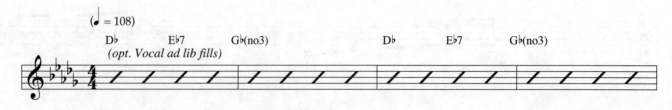

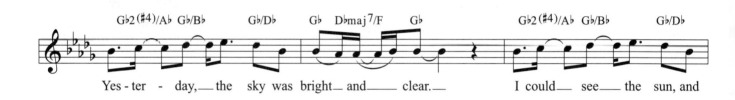

Yes-ter-day,__ the sky was bright__ and__ clear.__ I could__ see__ the sun, and

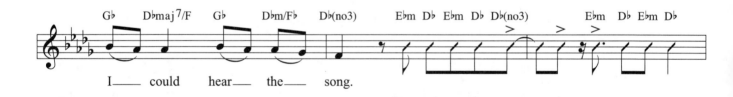

I____ could__ hear__ the__ song.

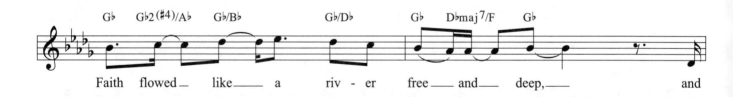

Faith flowed__ like__ a riv-er free__ and__ deep,____ and

grace was__ not__ so hard to__ be be-lieved;__ but that was yes-

© Copyright 2001 (Arr. © Copyright 2010) Sparrow Song (BMI) (Administered by EMI CMG Publishing) / Primary Wave Brian (Chapman Sp Acct.).
All rights reserved. Used by permission. Reprinted by permission of Hal Leonard Corporation.

Undo Me

Words and Music by
JENNIFER KNAPP

Pa-pa, — I think I messed up a-gain. — Was it some-thin' I did, or was it some-

-thin' I — said? — I don't mean to do — you wrong. — It's just the way —

— of hu-man na-ture. Sis-ter, — I know I

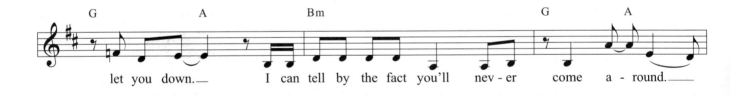

let you down. — I can tell by the fact you'll nev-er come a-round. —

You don't — have to say — a thing. — I can tell — by your eyes — ex-act-

-ly what you mean: — that it's time — to get down — on my knees — and pray: —

© Copyright 1998 Universal Music - Brentwood Benson Songs / West Hudson Music (BMI) (Licensing through Music Services). All rights reserved. Used by permission.

Wait for Me

Walking Her Home

529

Words and Music by
MARK SCHULTZ

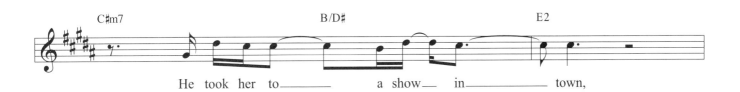

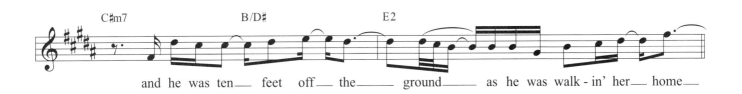

© Copyright 2003 CRAZY ROMAINE MUSIC (ASCAP) (Administered by The Loving Company). All rights reserved. Used by permission.

Welcome Home

Words and Music by
SHAUN GROVES

Take me, make me all You want me to be; that's all I'm ask-

-ing, all I'm ask - ing.

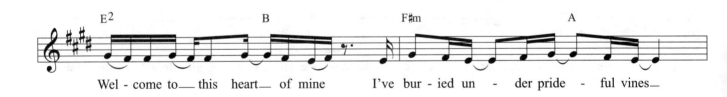
Wel - come to this heart of mine I've bur - ied un - der pride - ful vines

grown to hide the mess I've made in - side of me. Come dec - o - rate, Lord, and

o - pen up the creak - ing door and walk up - on the dust - y floor.

© Copyright 2001 New Spring, a division of Brentwood-Benson Music Publishing / Shaungroves.com (ASCAP) (Licensing through Music Services).
All rights reserved. Used by permission.

Who You Are

Words and Music by
JOSHUA MOORE

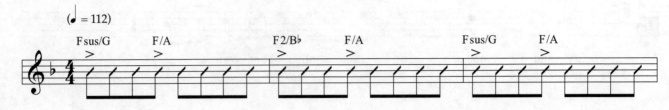

1. When I was young,___

You were my breath___ and___ heart - beat. Born in the dark,___

You were the hand___ that___ held___ me.

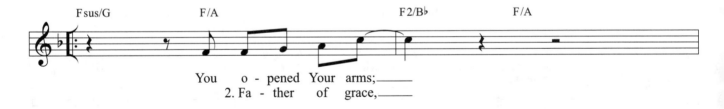
You o - pened Your arms;___
2. Fa - ther of grace,___

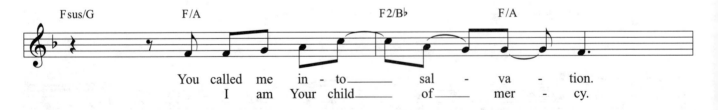
You called me in - to___ sal - va - tion.
I am Your child___ of___ mer - cy.

Your in - fi - nite love___
In - side my heart___

© Copyright 2001 Joshmooreownsthismusic (ASCAP) (Administered by Music Services). All rights reserved. Used by permission.

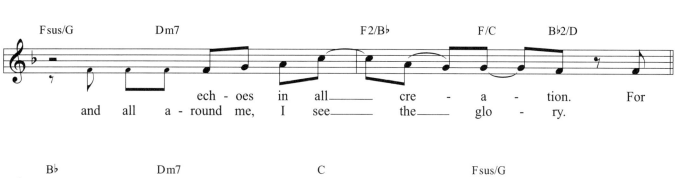

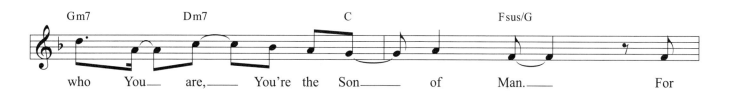

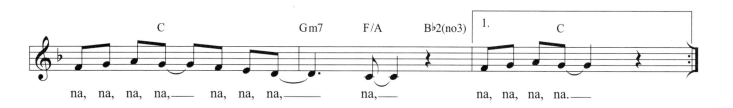
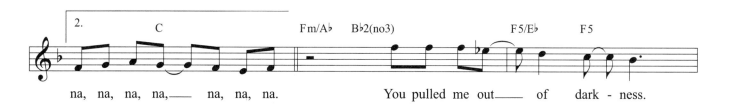
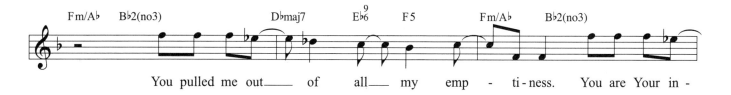

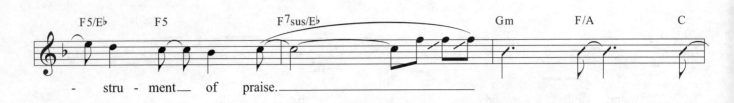

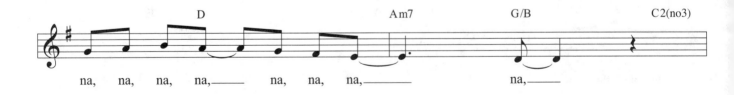
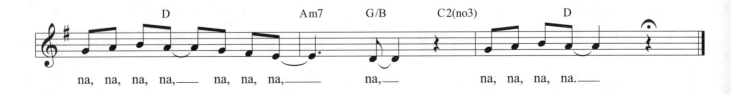

What If?

Words and Music by
NICHOLE NORDEMAN

© Copyright 2005 Birdwing Music / Birdboy Songs (ASCAP) (Administered by EMI CMG Publishing). All rights reserved. Used by permission.

Who Am I?

Words and Music by MARK HALL

Word of God, Speak

Words and Music by
BART MILLARD and PETE KIPLEY

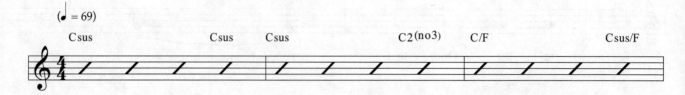
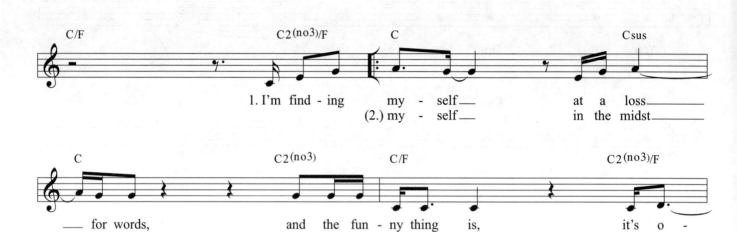
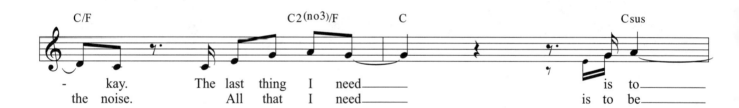
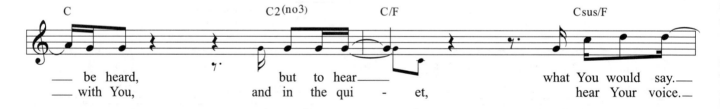
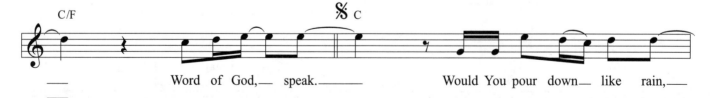
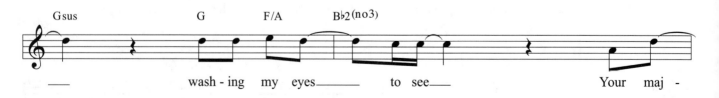

© Copyright 2002 Simpleville Music (ASCAP) (Administered by Simpleville Music, Inc.) /
Songs From the Indigo Room (Administered by Wordspring Music, LLC) / Wordspring Music, LLC.
All rights reserved. Used by permission.

Yes, I Believe

569

Words and Music by
JOEL LINDSEY and TONY WOOD

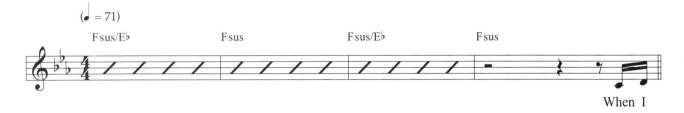

© Copyright 2001 New Spring, a division of Brentwood-Benson Music Publishing / Vacation Boy Music (ASCAP) (Licensing through Music Services).
All rights reserved. Used by permission.

You're My God

591

Words and Music by
JACI VELASQUEZ, MATTHEW GERRARD
and BRIDGET BENENATE

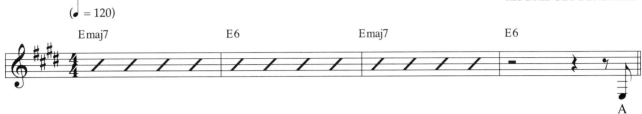

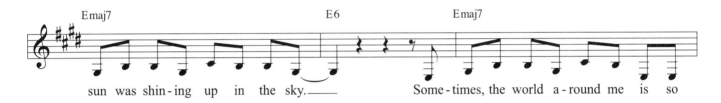

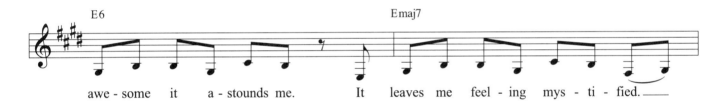

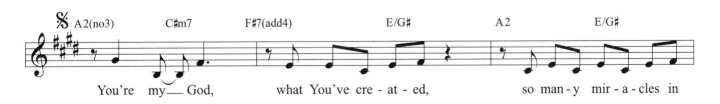

© Copyright 2003 (Arr. © Copyright 2010) Bug Music - Music of Windswept / Blotter Music / Friends of Seagulls Music Publishing /
WB Music Corp. / G. Matt Music / Jax and Broder Music (Administered by ION Music Administration). All rights on behalf of G. Matt Music
administered by WB Music Corp. All rights for Blotter Music and Friends of Seagulls Music Publishing administered by Bug Music - Music of Windswept.
All rights reserved. Used by permission. Reprinted by permission of Hal Leonard Corporation.

Your Grace Is Enough

Words and Music by
MATT MAHER

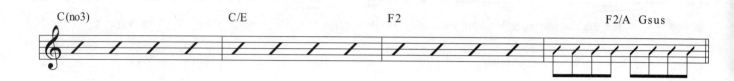

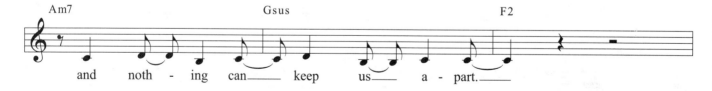

© Copyright 2004 Thankyou Music (PRS) (Administered worldwide by EMI CMG Publishing excluding Europe which is administered by kingswaysongs.com) / Spiritandsong.com ® (5536 NE Hassalo, Portland, OR 97213). All rights reserved. Used by permission.

Your Love, Oh Lord

Words and Music by
MAC POWELL, TAI ANDERSON, BRAD AVERY,
DAVID CARR and MARK LEE

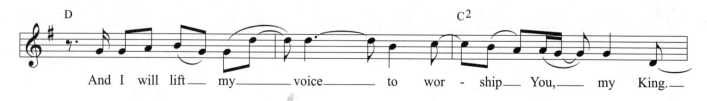

© Copyright 1999 New Spring, a division of Brentwood-Benson Music Publishing (ASCAP)
(Licensing through Music Services) / Vandura 2500 Songs (ASCAP) (Administered by EMI CMG Publishing).
All rights reserved. Used by permission.

40 Days----------2

A Baby's Prayer----------8
Above All----------5
Adonai----------10
Adore----------12
Alive, Forever, Amen----------18
All Because of Jesus----------20
All My Praise----------24
All That I Am----------15
Amazing, Because It Is----------34
Amazing Grace (My Chains Are Gone)----------26
Audience of One----------28
Awesome God----------32

Back in His Arms Again----------37
Be Still and Know----------40
Beautiful----------42
Beautiful One----------45
Better Is One Day----------48
Big Enough----------50
Big House----------53
Bless the Broken Road----------56
Blessed Be Your Name----------58
Breathe----------60
Butterfly Kisses----------63
By His Wounds----------66

Call on Jesus----------68
Can't Live a Day----------72
Cinderella----------78
Come Together----------82
Cover Me----------75
Cry Out to Jesus----------86

INDEX

Days of Elijah---92
Dead Man (Carry Me)---94
Deep Enough to Dream---96
Disappear---89
Dive---100
Don't Look at Me---104

East to West---110
Empty Me---124
Everlasting God---114
Every Move I Make---116
Everything Glorious---107
Everything to Me---120

Fearless---130
Find Your Wings---127
Flood---134
From the Inside Out---137

Gather at the River---140
Give It All Away---143
Give Me Words to Speak---146
Give Me Your Eyes---152
Glory Defined---149
God---156
God of This City---159
God of Wonders---162
God So Loved---165
God Speaking---168
God with Us---174
Grace Like Rain---178
Great Light of the World---171

INDEX

He Reigns---180
He Walked a Mile--183
He Will Carry Me--186
He's My Son---192
Healing Rain--196
Held--198
Here I Am to Worship--189
Here Is Our King--200
Here with Me--205
Hide--202
Holy--211
Holy Is the Lord--214
Holy Is Your Name---208
Homesick--216
Hope to Carry On--219
How Can I Keep from Singing?--222
How Great Is Our God--224

I Am--226
I Am Free---230
I Believe---232
I Can Only Imagine--236
I Choose You--240
I Could Sing of Your Love Forever---235
I Need You--247
I Need You to Love Me---250
I Still Believe---244
I Surrender All---252
I Will Rise---258
I'm Letting Go--255
I'm Not Who I Was---262
I've Always Loved You---267
If We Are the Body--264

INDEX

If You Want Me To	273
In Christ Alone (Koch)	279
In Christ Alone (Getty/Townend)	285
Indescribable	270
It Is You	276
Jesus Freak	288
Joy	282
King of Glory	292
Lead Me On	299
Leaving 99	302
Legacy	304
(Let It) Fade	308
Let My Words Be Few	310
Let Us Pray	296
Letters from War	314
Lifesong	318
Live 4 Today	324
Live for You	328
Living Water	321
Love Is Here	331
Made to Worship	334
Magnificent Obsession	341
Me and Jesus	338
Mighty to Save	346
More	349
(There's Gotta Be) More to Life	352
Mountain of God	355
My Heart Goes Out	358
My Savior, My God	362

INDEX

Never Alone---368
Never Going Back to OK---365
Nothing Compares---372
Nothing Without You---375

Ocean Floor---378
On My Knees---384
Once Again---381
One of These Days---386
Only Grace---390
Open the Eyes of My Heart---393
Orphans of God---396

People Get Ready (Jesus Is Coming)---398
Place in This World---400
Praise You in This Storm---405
Psalm 112---408

Ready for You---402
Ready to Fly---412
Redeemer---415
Revelation Song---418
Right Here---423

Say Won't You Say---420
Serious---426
Show Me Your Glory---430
Show You Love---435
Sing Alleluia---432
So Long, Self---438
Something Beautiful---441
Spoken For---444
Stand in the Rain---446

INDEX

Stomp----------448
Strong Tower----------453
Surrender----------456

Take You Back----------460
Tears of the Saints----------464
Testify to Love----------468
The Glory of the Blood----------471
The Motions----------474
The Other Side of the Radio----------476
The Valley Song (Sing of Your Mercy)----------483
The Wonderful Cross----------480
There Will Be a Day----------489
There You Go----------486
This Day----------494
This Is Your Time----------498
This Man----------501
Turn----------507

Undo----------510
Undo Me----------512
Unspoken----------504
Untitled Hymn (Come to Jesus)----------519

Voice of Truth----------522

Wait for Me----------516
Walking Her Home----------529
Watching Over Me----------526
We Live----------534
Welcome Home----------538
Welcome to Our World----------545
What If?----------546

INDEX

Who Am I?	548
Who I Am Hates Who I've Been	552
Who You Are	542
Wholly Yours	556
Witness	559
Wonder Why	566
Wonderful, Merciful Savior	562
Word of God, Speak	564
Yes, I Believe	569
You Are a Child of Mine	572
You Are Everything	576
You Are My King (Amazing Love)	582
You Found Me	578
You Never Let Go	588
You Raise Me Up	585
You Reign	594
You Were There	596
You're My God	591
Your Grace Is Enough	600
Your Love, Oh Lord	606
Your Name	604

INDEX